DESERTS

BIOMES OF NORTH AMERICA

Lynn M. Stone

Rourke

Publishing LLC

Vero Beach, Florida 32964

www.rourkepublishing.com

PHOTO CREDITS: All photos © Lynn M. Stone

Title page: *Desert habitats are homes for many lizards, including the poisonous gila monster.*

Editor: Frank Sloan

Cover and interior design by Nicola Stratford

Library of Congress Cataloging-in-Publication Data

Stone, Lynn M.
  Deserts / Lynn M. Stone.
     p. cm. — (Biomes of North America)
Summary: Looks at the deserts of the southwestern United States, animals that dwell in them, and how deserts are changing.
Includes bibliographical references (p.   ).
  ISBN 1-58952-683-X (hardcover)
  1. Deserts—Southwest, New—Juvenile literature. 2. Desert ecology—Southwest, New—Juvenile literature. [1. Deserts—Southwest, New. 2. Desert ecology. 3. Ecology.] I. Title. II. Series: Stone, Lynn M. Biomes of North America.
  QH104.5.S6S77 2003
  577.54'0979—dc21

                                                        2003004218

Printed in the USA

CG/CG

Table of Contents

Arctic Circle

Canada

United States

Cuba

Mexico

North American Desert

| 0 | | | 1500 | KM |
| 0 | | | 1000 | MILES |

Desert

Southwestern Deserts

The warm, or hot, deserts of the southwestern United States cover an area about the size of California and Montana combined. Much of north central and northwest Mexico is also desert.

Certain cold, dry areas in northern North America are sometimes called "polar" deserts. This book is only about the hot, southwestern deserts.

One desert can be quite different from another. A desert may be 5,000 feet (1,524 meters) above sea level or several feet below sea level. Deserts have different plants and animals. But deserts also share several important features. The main one is dryness.

Deserts have total rainfall of less than 10 inches (26 centimeters) in an average year.

Most deserts lie in huge basins surrounded by mountains. The mountains stop the flow of wet clouds and help keep deserts dry. Steady winds dry out the air and ground.

The distant Ajo mountains rise above Organ Pipe National Monument, Arizona.

The Desert Community

The deserts are **communities** of living things. Each living thing in the deserts depends on some of the others in one way or another. Plants, for example, are the basic food source for desert animals. Plants grow by using sunlight, soil, and water for food. Animals, in turn, grow by eating the plants, or by eating animals that eat plants.

Even a **predator**, like a coyote, snake, or hawk, depends upon desert plants. Why? Because the predator's **prey**, such as a ground squirrel, lives on plants. Without plants there would be no prey— and no predators.

The tiger rattlesnake is one of the desert's top predators.

Desert communities are homes, or habitats, for the things that live there. But living in the hot, dry deserts requires special ways to survive. Cactus plants, for example, store water in their fleshy stems.

Always alert for predators, a Yuma antelope squirrel sits on top of a spiny cactus branch.

Desert Animals

Desert animals come in many forms and sizes, from tiny insects to the mountain lion and desert bighorn sheep. The desert is also home for such animals as hummingbirds, elf owls, badgers, coyotes, deer, vultures, doves, and a variety of lizards and snakes. But big or small, desert animals have special ways to live in the harsh desert climate.

The plant-eating desert bighorn is the largest of North American desert animals.

One way to live is to avoid heat and to feed at night. Summer days are too hot even for desert animals. Most of them avoid summer heat by staying underground until nightfall. Others hide in shaded canyons or under brush.

Some desert animals, such as bighorns, find water in springs. But most desert animals take water from plants or their prey. Certain desert **rodents** can even make water from dry food!

16

A rock squirrel peeks out from under a rock, where it has been hiding from the hot desert sun.

The Changing Desert

Nature changes the North American deserts and people change them, too. Nature's changes don't harm the deserts. Nature's changes come with the seasons. Sudden bursts of rain bring millions of flower seeds to blossom in spring and summer wildflower gardens. And each spring cactus and brittlebush begin to bloom.

Cool weather means more animals are active by day. Cold weather forces some animals to **hibernate** or hide for days at a time.

Spring arrives on the Sonoran Desert in March with the blooms of Mexican gold poppies.

People have destroyed some of the deserts for cities and roads. But people have also **conserved** great parts of desert. Some of North America's finest examples of deserts are in Saguaro National Park, Organ Pipe National Monument, Great Basin National Park, and Death Valley National Park.

Spring blooms of owl-clover carpet Organ Pipe National Monument.

Spiky Joshua trees are typical of the Mojave Desert. Burros, brought to the desert by miners, have multiplied and threaten desert plants.

Glossary

communities (kuh MYU nuht eez) — habitats, or homes, for plants and animals

conserved (kon SERVD) — saved for future use or enjoyment

hibernate (HIGH ber nayt) — to enter into a sleeplike state for a lengthy period during cold months

predator (PRED uh tur) — an animal that kills other animals for food

prey (PRAY) — an animal that is killed by another animal for food

rodents (ROHD entz) — mammals that gnaw, including rats, mice, squirrels, beavers, and others

INDEX

Further Reading

Gray, Susan. *Deserts*. Compass Point Books, 2001
Johnson, Rebecca L. *Walk in the Desert*. Carolrhoda Books, 2001
Trumbauer, Lisa. *What Are Deserts?* Pebble Books, 2002
Wilkins, Sally. *Deserts*. Bridgestone Books, 2001

Websites To Visit

www.kidskonnect.com/Desert/DesertHome.html
www.yahooligans.com/Science_and_Nature

About The Author

Lynn Stone is a talented natural history photographer and writer. Lynn, a former teacher, travels worldwide to photograph wildlife in their natural habitat. He has more than 500 children's books to his credit.